Fluffy, The Neighborhood Dog

Written by: Kathy McClure

McPub™ Kids

An Entity of
McClure Publishing, Inc.

DEDICATION

This book is dedicated to my Grandchildren Bryce, Sinia; John (Jay); Chase, Lahya Sky, Noah Jaceyon, Carter, Mila, and Leonardo 'Leo' encouraging them to read and read some more.

Published in the United States by McClure
Publishing, Inc., Bloomingdale, IL, 800.659.4908
http://www.mcpubkids.com
books@mcpubkids.com

Illustrator: David Sanders

Editor: Rosie Cook
RosieCookC@aol.com

Library of Congress Catalog Number: 2014906398

Printed in the United States

ACKNOWLEDGEMENT

I would like to acknowledge children who have pets that they love and care for to keep them happy by playing, feeding, giving them plenty of water, taking them for walks, and keeping up with their visits at the Veterinary (pet hospital).

The Beginning

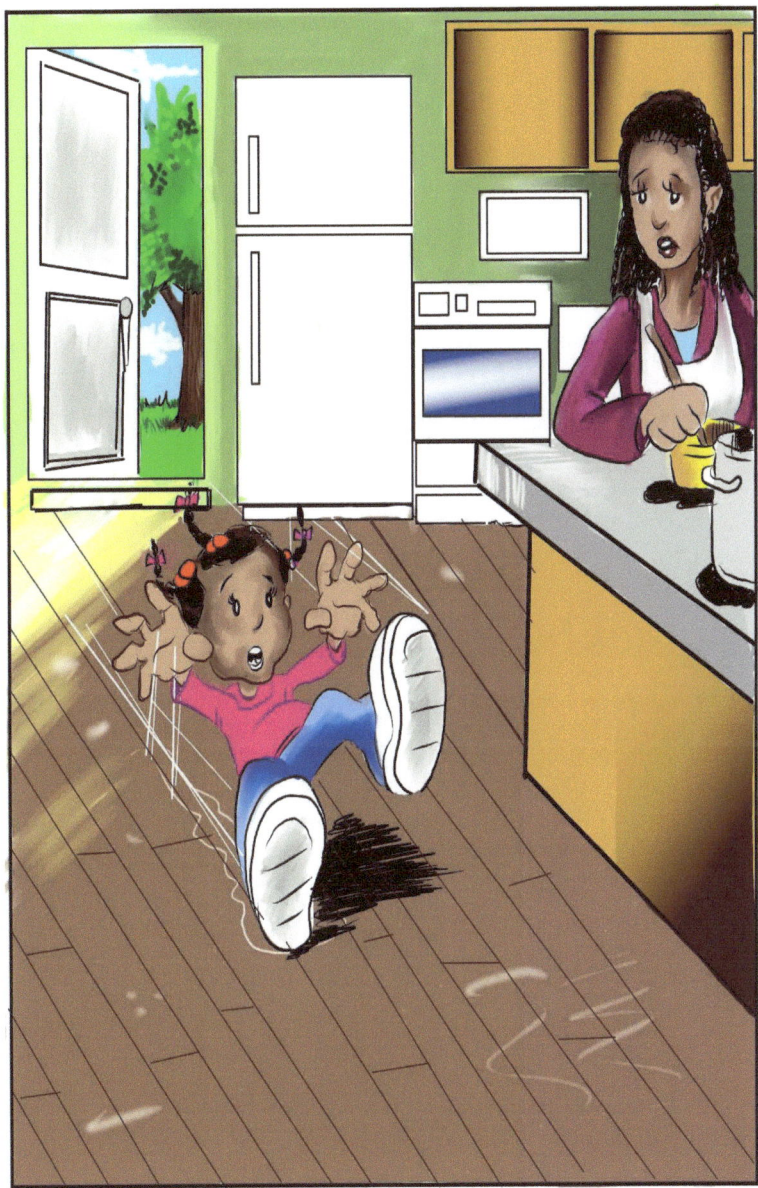

Katrina ran into the house. She ran so fast that she slid on the slippery wooden floor. "Mom, mom, come quickly," she said excitedly. "You really have to come and see what's going on outside."

"Katrina, what's wrong?" Mom asked sounding concerned.

"Something really bad has happened. Please hurry," Katrina pleaded.

Fluffy was helping a little boy get out of the street and a car hit him.

Mom was preparing dinner and laid her towel down on the counter. She rushed out the door with Katrina.

Katrina was very upset because she loves Fluffy. She tried calling him, but he didn't respond. She wondered what had gotten into Fluffy. Why wasn't he listening to her?

The car had turned the corner really fast. It caught Katrina off guard and before she knew it, Fluffy was in the street. When the car hit him, it made such a loud noise that everyone ran outside to see what had happened. Katrina's mom was so busy in the kitchen that she didn't hear the noise.

Katrina started crying. She clutched her stomach and bent over in pain. Mom kneeled down so that she could comfort her daughter. She reached in her other pocket, pulled out some napkins, and wiped Katrina's eyes.

Mom said, "Not to worry Katrina, Fluffy will be alright he has gone on to be in a better place."

What place could be better than here with me? Katrina thought.

"Fluffy entered into another place that was waiting for him to come," Mom said.

Katrina didn't understand what her mother meant; but she knew it sounded good.

Mom took Katrina inside the house to call 311. *Why would mom be calling 311?* Katrina wondered. She stood quietly while listening to what her mom was saying.

"I'm calling to report that a neighbor's dog was hit by a car and is lying in the middle of the street." Mom said. "I think the dog is badly hurt, but I'm not sure."

As Katrina listened, she started crying again. Mom asked if they could send someone immediately to see about the neighbor's dog. Katrina wasn't sure about the answer her mother received. What she did know was that the answer made her mother pretty upset. Katrina's mom started frowning while shaking her head.

Mom tried her best not to show her emotions. She quickly looks over at Katrina and forces a smile on her face as if everything was okay.

Mom could see in her mind the times that Katrina and Fluffy would be running and playing outside together.

"Katrina, are the neighbors home?" Mom asked.

"No," Katrina said. "They left earlier to go to the store to buy Fluffy some dog food. Katrina was growing tearful again and said, "When they get back, they won't need the food, will they, Mom? Mom, will someone come and get Fluffy out of the street?"

"Sure Katrina. They will come and take care of Fluffy," mom assured her.

Katrina was only 8 years old, and she didn't understand. She kept looking out of the window watching for Mr. and Mrs. McNabb to return from the store.

She saw a neighbor standing in the middle of the street at the corner to stop traffic from coming down the block. Another neighbor went into her house to get a blanket to cover Fluffy.

All the neighbors loved Fluffy because he was the dog that protected everyone. He wouldn't let anyone hurt the children on the block. Fluffy and Katrina was really close. They played all the time together.

When the McNabbs returned home, the other neighbors were saddened to have to tell them that Fluffy had been hit by a car.

The McNabbs jumped out of their car leaving the vehicle in the middle of the street and ran toward Fluffy.

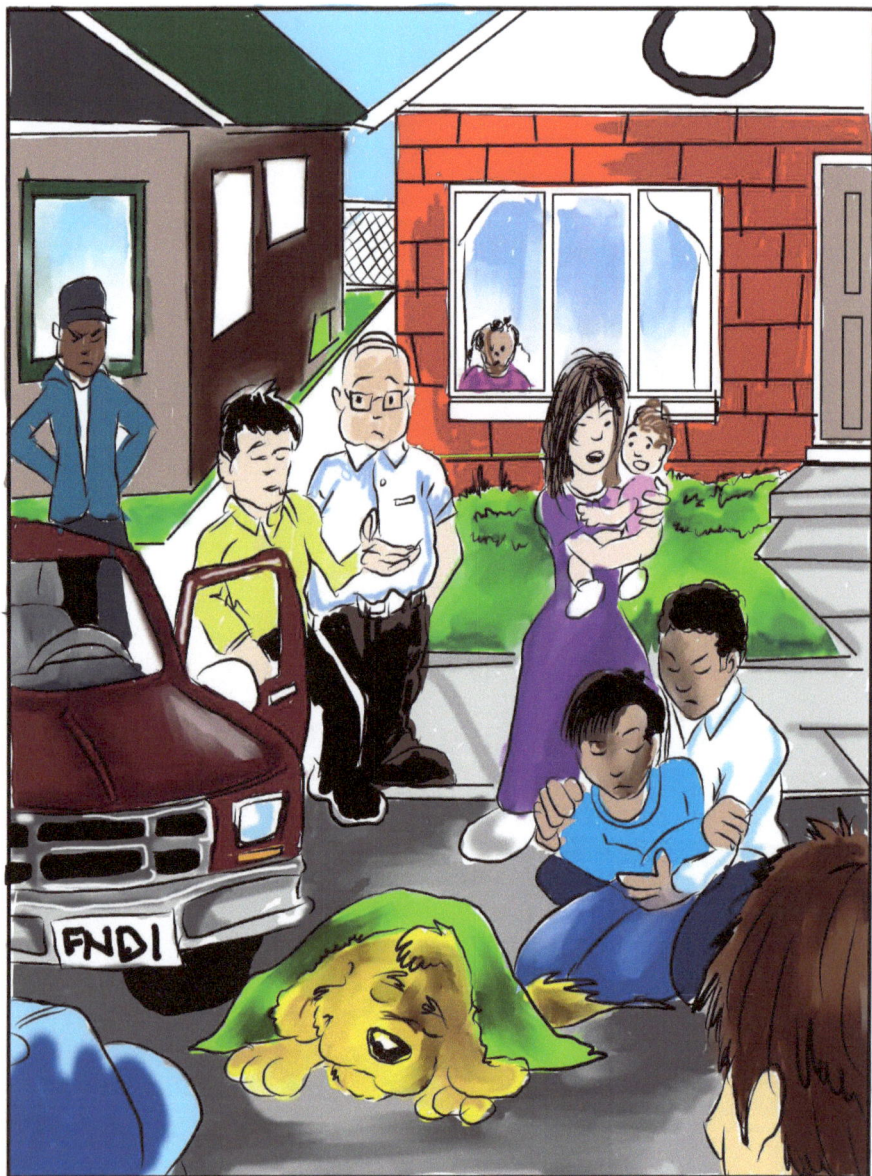

Mrs. McNabb fell to the ground and started screaming loudly saying, "No no no" while crying uncontrollably. Mr. McNabb bent down to comfort his wife. It was awful.

Mrs. Smyth, one of the neighbors, ran into the street to tell them what had happened.

"I'm so sorry," she said. "I saw my child running into the street, and I couldn't react fast enough. Then suddenly Fluffy ran into the street and the car hit him.

Fluffy saved my child's life. He saw the car coming before I did. By the time I saw the car it would've been too late. The car was going so fast that I wouldn't have gotten to my baby in time."

The neighbor cried so much that she passed out. When she finally came to, the other neighbors got her up from the ground.

A week after Fluffy's accident, Katrina's mom sat at the kitchen table peeling potatoes. She was making hamburgers and fries for dinner. That was her daughter's favorite meal, and she was hoping it would cheer her up.

Katrina hadn't really been herself after Fluffy got hurt. For the past three days, she would come home from school, finished her homework, ate dinner, helped her mom with the dishes, and then rushed to her room to work on what she called her "special project."

One Evening Katrina's mom looked up from slicing the potatoes and saw Katrina standing in the doorway of the kitchen.

"Hi, sweetheart," her mother said, smiling. "What's up?"

"I finished my project," Katrina said, with her hands behind her back as she walked toward her mother.

"Oh, that's great," her mom said, cutting the potatoes into very thin slices, just the way Katrina liked them. "Which class is it for?"

"Well," Katrina said. "It isn't for a class." She paused. "It's for Fluffy."

Her mother looked at her with a puzzled expression, and said, "Fluffy?"

Katrina nodded. She slowly brought her hands from behind her back and presented her mother with a sheet of paper.

Mom wiped her hands on the towel that was on the table and reached for the paper from her daughter. Printed very neatly and in bright, colorful letters, she read out loud what Katrina had written.

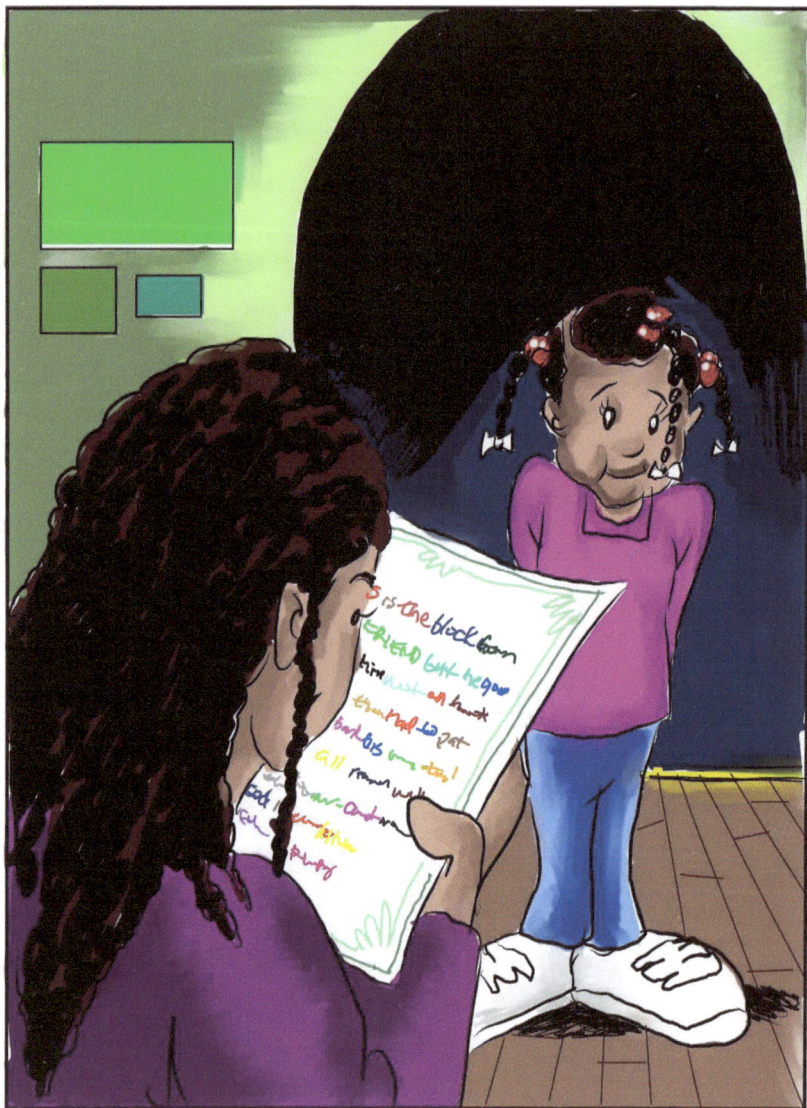

This is the block where Fluffy was born.

He was our friend but now he's gone.

Everyone loved him with all our hearts.

He saved a life, and then had to part.

His happy bark, his wagging tail

Are things we all remember well.

Though we can't see him with our eyes,

He'll always be with us deep, down inside.

You will be missed Fluffy!
We Love You!

Katrina's mother blinked tears as she stared down at the poem her daughter had written, imagining how much time it took her to write each word so neatly and in a different color with her markers. She looked up at her daughter and smiled proudly. "It's beautiful," she said. "Not only is it beautiful to *hear*, but it's beautiful to *look* at too."

Katrina smiled, basking in the glow of her mother's praise.

"I want to give it to the McNabbs," Katrina said. "Do you think they'll like it, mom?"

Her mother stared at her; the love for her daughter shining in her eyes. "No," she said, shaking her head from side to side.

Katrina's smile quickly dropped from her face at her mother's answer.

"I think they will absolutely *love* it," her mother said, smiling.

Katrina's smile returned, even wider, as her mother rose from the table, pulled her daughter into her arms, and hugged her tightly.

Encircled in the warmth of her mother's love, Katrina thought about Fluffy. She closed her eyes and imagined him barking happily and wagging his tail in that "better place" where her mother said Fluffy had gone.

The phone rang and Katrina's mom answered. It is the McNabbs with news about Fluffy.

Mr. McNabb exclaimed, "We are calling to let you know that Fluffy will be home in a few days. The car knocked the wind out of him, but by the time he got to see the Veterinarian, he was breathing and was just a little groggy."

Katrina's mom was happy to know and excitedly shared the great news with Katrina.

When Fluffy got home, Katrina did not want to put him on the floor.

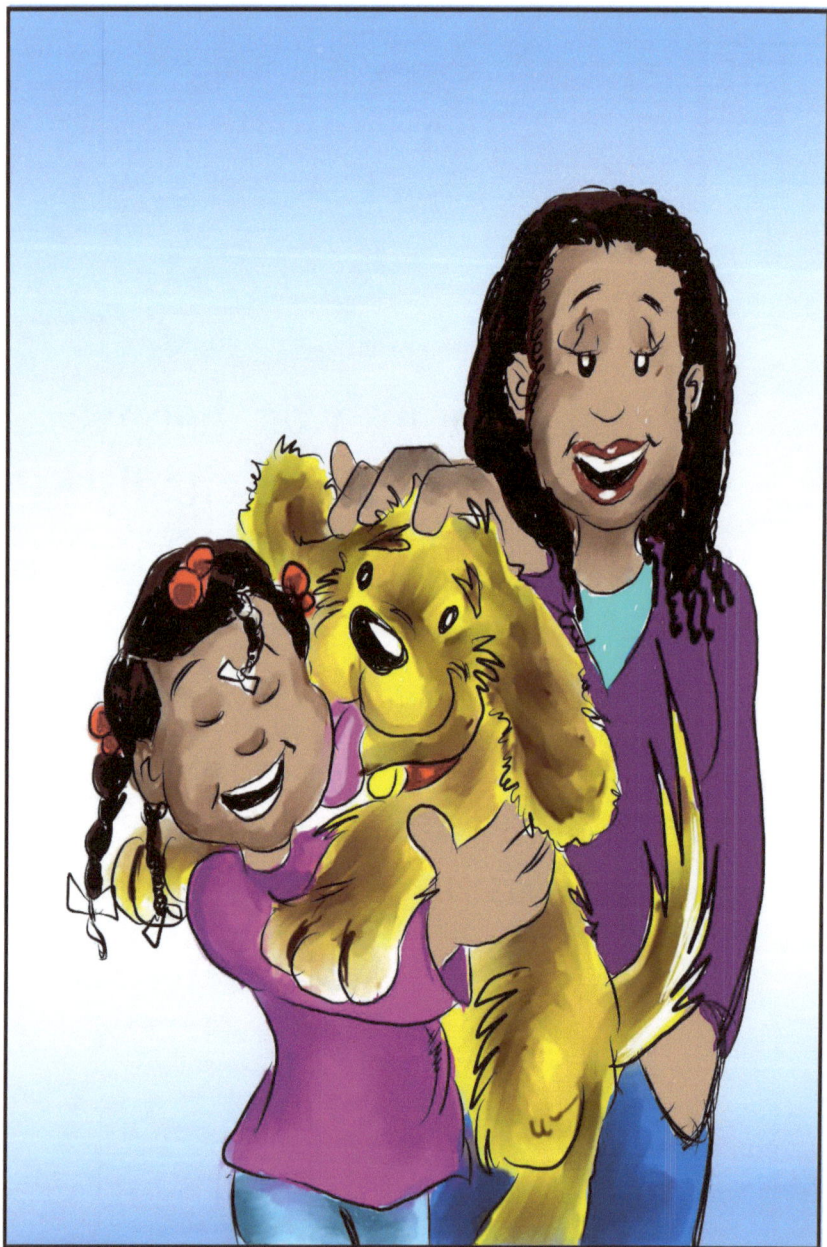

The End

Fluffy, The Neighborhood Dog has a 1st edition which is more of a reality. I thought it would be nice to turn the book into a cartoon look for children in the 2nd edition.

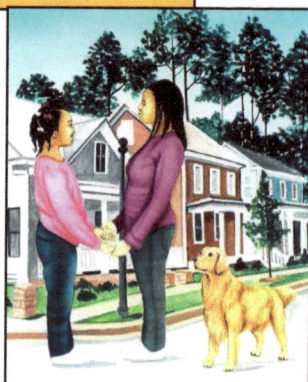

MOMENTS OF KATRINA AND FLUFFY 2ND EDITION